Rocks, Gems, and Minerals

Rocks, Gems, and Minerals

Trudi Strain Trueit

Franklin Watts
A Division of Scholastic Inc.
New York • Toronto • London • Auckland • Sydney
Mexico City • New Delhi • Hong Kong
Danbury, Connecticut

For Marie, a rare and precious jewel

Note to readers: Definitions for words in **bold** can be found in the Glossary at the back of this book.

Photographs © 2003: Earth Scenes: 33 top (Dani/Jeske), 17 top left, 22 top left (E.R. Degginger), 5 right, 16, 21 top, 21 bottom, 23 top left, 23 bottom right (Breck P. Kent), 18 bottom (Michael Thompson); Peter Arnold Inc./Ed Reschke: 2; Photo Researchers, NY: 43 (Bill Belknap), 15 bottom (Robert de Gugliemo/SPL), 28 top (Gregory G. Dimijian), 14 (Adam Hart-Davis/SPL), 9 (Cheryl Hogue), 5 left, 37 (Adam Jones), 38 (Geoff Lane/CSIRO/SPL), 35 (Andrew J. Martinez), 24 (Tom McHugh), 8 (Will and Deni McIntyre), 17 bottom (Astrid & Hans-Frieder Michler/SPL), 30 (Richard T. Nowitz), 15 top left (Pekka Parviainen/SPL), 22 top right (Mark A. Schneider); Stock Boston: 6 (Walter Bibikow), 17 top right, 23 top right (Stephen Frisch); Superstock, Inc.: 28 bottom (Ron Dahlquist), 12 (Silvio Fiore), 29 (Dwayne Harlan), 32 (Tom Murphy), 31 (Graeme Outerbridge), cover (Peter Van Rhijn), 10 (Steve Vidler), 40, 41; Unicorn Stock Photos/Eric R. Berndt: 19; Visuals Unlimited: 15 top right (Cabisco), 18 top (Kevin Collins), 22 bottom right, 23 bottom left (A.J. Copley), 33 bottom (Gerald & Buff Corsi), 26 (Jonn D. Cunningham), 47 (Mark E. Gibson), 22 bottom left (Mark A. Schneider), 45 (Tom Uhlman).

The photograph on the cover shows rock formations along the shore of Georgian Bay in Ontario, Canada. The photograph opposite the title page shows limestone sedimentary rock formations in Bryce Canyon, Utah.

Library of Congress Cataloging-in-Publication Data

Trueit, Trudi.
    Rocks, gems, and minerals / Trudi Strain Trueit.
        p. cm. – (Watts Library)
    Includes bibliographical references and index.
    ISBN 0-531-12195-X (lib. bdg.)   0-531-16241-9 (pbk.)
    1. Rocks—Juvenile literature. 2. Minerals—Juvenile literature. 3. Precious stones—Juvenile literature. [1. Rocks. 2. Minerals. 3. Precious stones.] I. Title. II. Series.
QE432.2.T78 2003
552—dc2

12001007222

Contents

Chapter One
World of Wonders   7

Chapter Two
Mineral Magic 13

Chapter Three
The Circle of Stone 27

Chapter Four
Hot on the Mineral Trail 39

Chapter Five
Where Do You Stand? 45

48 **Glossary**

55 **To Find Out More**

59 **A Note on Sources**

61 **Index**

This glass pyramid serves as the main entrance to the famed Louvre museum in Paris, France. Created by architect I. M. Pei, the pyramid is made of interlinked steel sheathed in reflective glass.

Chapter One

World of Wonders

Under the scorching Egyptian sun, hundreds of stonecutters chipped holes into giant slabs of limestone. After inserting wood into the holes, the workers poured water over them. When the wet wood expanded, the rocks splintered into pieces. Sculptors then chiseled the white chunks into blocks. One by one, the stones were towed up a mud ramp on a sled. Each heavy rock had to be carefully set in place by hand. The grueling work took more than twenty years to complete,

Big Building Blocks

There are 2.3 million stones in the Great Pyramid, each weighing between 2 and 15 tons.

but when the Great Pyramid of King Khufu was finally finished, its golden tip rose 481 feet (147 meters) above the sands of Giza.

Four thousand years ago, the workers constructing the Great Pyramid believed they were creating a sacred tomb that would allow their pharaoh to pass from this life into the next. They had no way of knowing the monument, along with three smaller pyramids built nearby, would survive desert winds, blowing sand, pollution, and grave robbers to become one of the seven wonders of the ancient world—and the only one still standing today.

For thousands of years, humans have used rocks and minerals for construction, weapons, jewelry, tools, and money. Over time, our reliance on rock has deepened. Today, we look to stones to provide us with such necessities as glass windows, steel bridges, and concrete roads. Mineral crystals keep telephones, clocks, computers, and appliances running smoothly. Metals such as aluminum, iron, and lead help produce airplanes and cars. Gold, diamonds, and other jewels are mined for a worldwide gem market. Just as stones gave shape to the pyramids in Egypt, they have given rise to many other amazing structures, including England's Stonehenge, the

The ancient monument of Stonehenge, on the Salisbury Plain in England, has mystified viewers for centuries. Although no one knows for sure, it was probably built thousands of years ago as a temple or astronomical observatory.

The Great Wall of China is probably the largest stone construction in human history.

Great Wall of China, and even a modern-day pyramid—the glass addition built onto France's Louvre Museum in 1989.

While rocks may seem solid and unchanging, nothing could be further from the truth. The forces of nature on Earth are always at work, forming new rock even as they are

House of Stone

From the cement foundation to the slate tiles covering the roof, a home is filled with things made from rocks and minerals: copper electrical wiring and pipes, metal nails and screws, brick fireplaces, marble and granite countertops, aluminum blinds and rain gutters, paint, and porcelain (clay) tiles, sinks, and toilets.

breaking down older rock. This never-ending **geologic cycle**, or **rock cycle**, is continually **recycling** Earth's crust. It may take millions of years for even the smallest changes to occur, yet this time-consuming journey has much to tell **geologists**, scientists who study the rocks and structure of planets, about Earth's past and future.

Fireworks are just one of an infinity of uses humankind has developed for minerals.

Chapter Two

Mineral Magic

Crack! Boom! Splashes of red and blue light up the night sky. Onlookers "ooh" and "aah" at the sight, perhaps unaware that the burst and bang of fireworks come from **minerals**. Minerals are solid forms of one or more chemical **elements** that occur naturally on Earth. Copper (Cu) salts make blue sparks, barium (Ba) salts produce green, sodium (Na) creates yellow, and strontium (Sm) gives off a red shower. The minerals are made into colored pellets, called stars. The stars are packed into tubes or round shells along with gunpowder, which contains the mineral sulfur. The gunpowder sends the

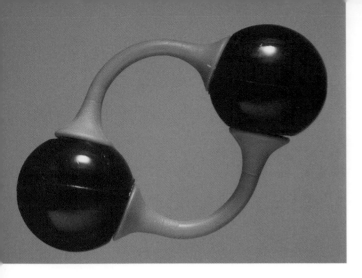

This is a computer model of a molecule of oxygen, one of Earth's most common elements. The model shows two oxygen atoms (the red spheres) joined by a double bond.

firework skyward, where it explodes in a blaze of color.

Minerals are made up of chemical elements. There are more than one hundred known elements on Earth. Oxygen (O) and silicon (Si) are two of the most common elements, while aluminum (Al), iron (Fe), calcium (Ca), sodium, potassium (K), and magnesium (Mg) are found in far smaller amounts. These eight elements make up almost all matter, including 99 percent of the rock found in Earth's crust.

Some minerals such as gold (Au), copper, or sulfur (S) can be formed by a single element. Most minerals are made up of two or more elements that bond to form a **chemical compound**. There is probably a mineral in your freezer right now. Two **atoms** (the very smallest parts of elements) of the element hydrogen (H) and one atom of oxygen (O) combine to form water (H_2O). When frozen, H_2O becomes a solid mineral known as ice.

When the atoms in one or more elements connect they create a **crystal**, which is a solid mineral body with a distinctive

Fireworks of the Future

The latest craze in fireworks goes beyond the usual flower shapes. The explosions now form hearts, stars, and smiley faces. Computer chips have fireworks doing more spectacular stunts, such as writing names across the night sky, and even creating portraits.

Frost "flowers" on a window (above) consist of large crystals of ice.

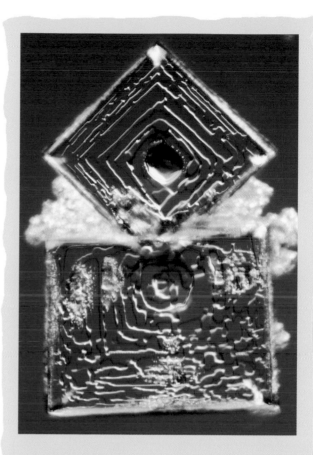

Pass the Salt

Separately, the elements sodium (Na) and chlorine (Cl) are poisonous, but together they create the mineral halite (NaCl) and become something you don't think twice about sprinkling on your french fries—table salt. The photo above shows a salt crystal.

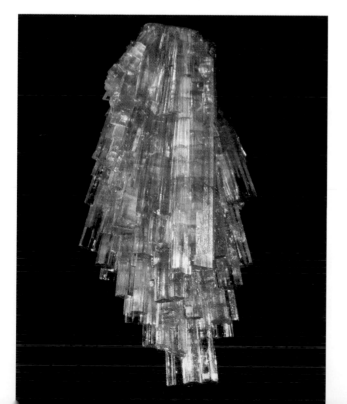

Tourmaline (left) actually exists as several different but closely related minerals. Tourmaline is known for its rich and varied colors, including black, brown, blue, green, red, and pink.

structure. Tourmaline contains fourteen elements, making it one of the most complex and colorful of all minerals. A single tourmaline crystal may have as many as fifteen colors in shades of green, red, pink, white, brown, and black.

A Firm Foundation

If you've ever inspected a **rock** closely, you've probably noticed the tiny, colored speckles on its surface. Those bits are minerals. The mineral crystals have either grown together or have grown separately and been cemented together. Rocks can be made up of just one mineral, many minerals, or a mixture of minerals and other **organic matter**, which is the remains of dead plants and animals.

There are more than four thousand known minerals in the world, but only about twenty-five create most types of rock. One of the most common minerals, quartz, is formed when the elements silicon and oxygen combine. Any mineral that contains at least these two elements is called a **silicate**. Micas, feldspars, and quartzes are groups of silicate minerals that can

This granite sample is from Barre, a town in north-central Vermont that is famous for its granite quarries.

Although feldspar is one of the most common minerals in Earth's crust, the green variety, also known as amazonite (left), is much rarer.

be found in various combinations in **granite**. A piece of granite might contain crystals of black mica, pink feldspar, clear quartz, or several combinations of other silicates. Feldspar is used to make porcelain and ceramic products such as sinks and bathtubs. Because quartz conducts electricity, it helps clocks and watches keep perfect time.

Minerals such as gold, silver (Ag), iron, copper, lead (Pb), mercury (Hg), uranium (U), zinc (Zn), platinum (Pt), and aluminum are metals. The most valuable metal is platinum, which is far more rare than gold. When different metal elements are combined they form **alloys**. The elements copper and zinc create the alloy brass, while copper and tin (Sn) make bronze.

Mercury has one of the most unique properties of any element: It is the only metal that is liquid at room temperature (above).

Zinc (below) is the 23rd-most abundant element in Earth's crust and stands fourth among all metals in worldwide production. It is also a necessary element for proper growth and development of humans, animals, and plants.

Copper, bronze, or brass were used to make this ancient Roman coin depicting the Emperor Hadrian (right) and these bells (below). The ability to forge and use these three metals represented a major step in humanity's development.

Nonmetallic minerals include halite and sylvite (rock salts), gypsum, calcite, graphite, sulfur, and fluorite. Gypsum goes into fertilizers, plaster, and cement. Calcite forms limestone, a rock that is used in buildings, statues, chalk, and cement. Graphite, when mixed with clay, is used in pencils. Sulfur is an ingredient in fertilizer and is used in the manufacturing of rubber. The fluoride in toothpaste comes from fluorite.

The gem minerals, such as beryl, corundum, and diamond, grow inside a host rock called a **matrix**. Diamonds grow in a matrix of kimberlite rock that forms more than 90 miles (140 km) underground at temperatures above 2,000° F (1,100° C). Made from a single element, carbon (C), diamonds are blown to the surface by volcanic eruptions. Corundum, which yields rubies and sapphires, is often found in marble, gneiss, and schist rock. Emeralds and aquamarines are cut from beryl crystals that grow in granite.

A construction worker spreads cement. Cement is a mixture of many elements, most commonly alumina, silica, lime, iron oxide, and magnesium oxide.

Crystals with Character

Of the thousands of minerals on Earth, no two are alike. Every mineral has its own recipe of chemical elements that is virtually the same, no matter where in the world the mineral is found. The atoms of these elements connect to develop a three-dimensional geometric shape or **crystal form**. There are six main shapes that crystals form: cube, tetragonal

Gems of the World

Mineral	Gem Produced	Places Found	Fun Facts
Beryl	Emerald	Brazil, Egypt, Colombia, China, Austria, United States	Egypt's Queen Cleopatra loved emeralds so much that in 50 BC she had her portrait engraved on one.
Corundum	Ruby	Myanmar, Thailand	Roman gladiators wore rubies, trusting the "blood stones" would stop their wounds from bleeding. Ancient Persians believed Earth was held up by a blue sapphire that was reflected above them in the sky.
	Sapphire	Australia, Canada, Sri Lanka	
Diamond	Diamond	Australia, South Africa, Russia, Venezuela	Legend says India's Hope Diamond carries a curse. Many of its owners, such as Marie Antoinette, died tragically. The diamond now rests in the Smithsonian Institution in Washington, DC.
Olivine	Peridot	United States (Arizona), Egypt, Myanmar, China	Most meteorites contain olivine and peridot. Apollo astronauts even discovered olivine in moon rocks.
Opal	Opal	Australia, Brazil, Mexico, Russia, United States	As much as 30 percent of an opal can be made of water (most are between 5 and 10 percent water). Rare black opals can be worth more than diamonds.
Quartz	Amethyst	Russia, India, Brazil	Ancient Egyptians carved scarab beetles out of amethyst to make good luck charms.

	Citrine	Argentina, Brazil, Madagascar, Scotland, Spain, United States	When heated, a purple amethyst becomes a gold citrine. Natural citrines are quite rare.
Topaz	Topaz	Brazil, Mexico, Russia, Ukraine, United States	In the 1960s, several blue topazes were discovered in Ukraine that weighed more than 200 pounds (90 kilograms) each

Amethyst specimen (above)

Talc specimen (below)

(stretched cube), triangular hexagon, monoclinic (rectangle set on end), orthorhombic (flat matchbox shape), and triclinic (irregular shape).

How the atoms are arranged in a mineral determines its **properties**, or characteristics. Geologists test for these properties when identifying a mineral. The most obvious property is color, but identifying a mineral by appearance alone can be tricky. Trace amounts of elements, called **impurities**, can tint a mineral and change its original color. Small iron particles can color clear quartz purple, creating amethyst, while other elements can turn it pink, white, or black. Pure corundum is clear. Traces of chromium will produce red rubies, while traces of iron and titanium will

21

Gypsum specimen

Calcite specimen

Fluorite specimen

Apatite specimen

produce blue sapphires. Since many of the gem minerals are colorless in their pure form, the most valuable diamonds, rubies, sapphires, and emeralds are those that have little or no color at all.

Orthoclase specimen

Quartz crystal specimen

Topaz specimen

Corundum specimen

Streak is the color produced when a mineral is rubbed against a piece of unglazed porcelain to make powder. This is more reliable than looking at a mineral's color to identify it because, no matter what color the weathered outside is, the

A diamond glimmers in a kimberlite matrix, which is how diamonds are found in nature. Kimberlite is a naturally occurring pipelike formation of different rocks.

smudges left behind are always the same color for a particular mineral. Some minerals even leave a smell behind when they are rubbed against porcelain. Sulfur smells like rotten eggs.

Luster is the way a mineral reflects light. Metal ores are said to have a metallic luster. Nonmetallic minerals are described as glassy, earthy (dull), silky, or pearly.

Durability is one of the most effective ways to identify a mineral. In 1812, German mineralogist Friedrich Mohs came up with a scale that tested ten different minerals for hardness based on how they resisted scratching. Each mineral on the **Mohs Scale** can scratch the one below it. Using this scale, the hardness of all minerals is classified from 0 to 10.

Diamond is the hardest naturally created mineral on Earth. It can scratch all other known minerals. A diamond's hardness makes it excellent for drilling, grinding, polishing, and for use in surgical instruments. Still, it is breakable. If you hit it just right with a hammer, a diamond will shatter.

Crystal Palace

In 1995, the Swarovski Company built Crystal Worlds near Innsbruck, Austria. Inside the museum, visitors can view a 36-foot (11-m) wall covered with 12 tons of crystals. They can also step inside a dome in which six hundred mirrors have been arranged to create the illusion that the visitors are in the center of a giant crystal.

Mohs Scale of Hardness

Hardness	Mineral	Common Tests	Description
1 2	Talc Gypsum	Can be scratched by a fingernail	Minerals below 2 are soft. Talc is used to make talcum powder. Evaporating seawater leaves gypsum behind.
3 4 5	Calcite Fluorite Apatite	Can be scratched by a copper coin Can be scratched by a knife blade or window glass	Minerals between 3 and 5 are medium. Calcite forms from the the shells of some animals, such as oysters and snails. Apatite is found in mammalian bones.
6 7 8 9	Orthoclase Quartz Topaz Corundum	Scratches a knife blade or window glass	Minerals above 6 are hard. Orthoclase is used in porcelain and ceramics. Topaz is twice as hard as quartz and corundum is twice as hard as topaz.
10	Diamond	Scratches all materials	Diamonds are four times harder than corundum. (Only a diamond can scratch a diamond.)

Scientists also use other specialized tests to look for properties within a mineral. Fluorite and biotite contain the element fluorine (F) and, when put under ultraviolet light, may sometimes glow. Minerals containing the elements uranium or plutonium are radioactive. Sulfur and quartz give off electrical charges when squeezed. Minerals such as hematite, pyrite, and magnetite contain iron and attract magnets.

Granite outcroppings such as these can be found on every continent. Granite is an igneous rock that is a tight interlocking of the minerals quartz, alkali feldspar, and plagioclase feldspar.

Chapter Three

The Circle of Stone

Have you ever left your footprint in rock? If you've strolled on the beach in your bare feet, you have done just that. The grains of sand that wriggled between your toes were made from larger rocks and shells that were worn down by weather, water, and chemicals. Just as nature is continually breaking rocks apart, it is also at work creating new rocks.

Geologists place rocks into three broad categories based on how they are

27

formed: **igneous**, **sedimentary**, and **metamorphic**. Igneous comes from the Latin word for fire. This type of rock is made when hot, melted (molten) rock called **magma** is cooled either above or below ground. Sedimentary rock, like the sand under your feet, comes from larger rocks that have been broken down and organic material. Metamorphic rock is made from igneous rock, sedimentary rock, and other metamorphic rock that has been changed over long periods of time by heat and/or pressure. This chapter will focus on how each of the three main types of rock is formed.

Strata of the metamorphic rocks marble, gneiss, and schist are seen above as deposits of sedimentary limestone and sandstone in the Sequoia National Forest in California. Lava from Kilauea volcano in Hawaii will become igneous rock.

Oozing Igneous Rock

Deep under Earth's surface, some of the planet's rocks are melting. The mineral "soup" flows into large **magma chambers** that feed volcanoes. The liquid is made up of many elements and gases. Because it is lighter than the rock around it, the magma begins to rise. On its upward journey, the magma may cool and harden between other rocks. Before it reaches the surface, it crystallizes to form a type of igneous rock called **plutonic rock**.

How the magma cools determines the type and size of the crystals that will grow from it. Each mineral has a certain temperature at which it crystallizes. Trapped beneath the surface of Earth, plutonic rock may spend tens of thousands of years cooling. This allows large crystals to form. Granite is one of the most common types of plutonic igneous rocks. Its minerals form large crystals. Huge magma blobs may produce giant masses of granite called **batholiths**. Millions of years of weather and other forces of nature, such as floods and earthquakes, may eventually wear away the overlying rock and expose a batholith that extends several hundred miles or more.

Granite is the building block for mountains such as Pikes Peak in the Colorado Rockies and Yosemite National Park in the Sierra Nevada Mountains. Since granite can handle the wear and tear of weather, it is used to construct buildings, roads, and statues. Other types of plutonic rock include diorite, gabbro, peridotite, and syenite.

Sometimes, if magma is extremely hot and a volcano's crust is split or shallow, molten rock will not cool inside Earth. Instead, it will continue up the volcanic pipeline, fueled by steam or water vapor, which is water in the form of gas. The bubbling liquid bursts out of the volcano. Once it reaches the

The stark granite face of El Capitan in Yosemite National Park is one of America's best-known landmarks.

Taken for Granite

Under the direction of sculptor Gutzon Borglum, four hundred workers spent fifteen years jack-hammering and dynamiting away 500,000 tons of granite to hand carve the 60-foot (18-m) busts of (from left) U.S. presidents George Washington, Thomas Jefferson, Theodore Roosevelt, and Abraham Lincoln into the cliffs at Mount Rushmore. Nature also played a major role in shaping the massive work of art. The angle of Lincoln's face had to be changed after a long crack was spotted running through his nose. Also, because of inconsistencies in the granite, Jefferson's head was moved from the right side of Washington to his left.

surface of the planet, magma is called **lava**. As the lava flows out of the volcano, it cools and solidifies into igneous **volcanic rock**. Unlike plutonic rock, which is slow to cool, volcanic rock exposed to the outside air cools rapidly. Only tiny crystals have time to grow, forming a very fine-grained rock. **Rhyolite** is a volcanic rock made from some of the same minerals as granite. If the lava on the surface cools too fast for any crystals to form, a shiny type of rock called obsidian is produced. This **volcanic glass** is easily polished and sharpened. Ancient people often fractured obsidian into blades, axes, sharp arrowheads, and other tools. Obsidian is usually dark brown or black in color, but may be speckled with white crystals or colored. Rainbow obsidian, with its purple, gold, and green stripes, is more rare and valuable than black obsidian.

Basalt is the most abundant volcanic rock. Formed from lava flows, basalt makes up more than half of Earth's crust, including the upper crust of the ocean floor. The rapid cooling of thick layers of basalt forms brown, hexagonal-shaped pillars such as those found at Giant's Causeway in Northern Ireland. Repeated volcanic eruptions can result in layers of

Light as a Rock?

The lava that forms pumice, a type of rhyolite, cools so quickly its gases don't have time to escape. Frothy gas bubbles create a rock that looks like a sponge. Pumice is so light, it often can float on water.

The Giant's Causeway in County Antrim, Ireland, is a mass of basalt columns packed tightly together and leading from the foot of a cliff to the sea. According to Irish folklore, the columns were placed there by the legendary Celtic giant Finn MacCool.

basalt up to 5 miles (8 kilometers) thick. These flood basalts flow great distances. Two large flood basalts are the Columbia Basin in Washington State and the Deccan traps of western India, which measures 200,000 square miles (500,000 sq km). The Hawaiian Islands, including the active Kilauea volcano, are also made of basalt.

Sedimentary Rocks on the Go

Sedimentary rocks are formed only on Earth's surface. They are made from bigger rocks and the remains of plants and animals that have broken down over time. Although you may not be able to see it, the Sun, wind, rain, and ice are slowly wearing away the face of the planet. Over millions of years, this **physical weathering** causes rock formations on the surface to break down. Rain may mix with carbon dioxide from the air, forming acid that can eat away rock. This is called **chemical weathering.** Decaying plants and animals also produce acids that are destructive to rock.

Bit by bit, particles of rock are chipped away and transported from one place to another through **erosion**. Floods, river flows, glaciers, ocean waves, and ocean currents are all forces and

This pinkish-toned sandstone is from the ancient Jordanian city of Petra. Sandstone is one of the most common of sedimentary rocks.

events that can erode rock. A piece of rock may travel a short distance or perhaps several hundred miles to become part of the ocean floor. **Deposition** occurs when eroded rock settles in a particular place. As layer after layer of rock is deposited in an area, the increasing weight presses the sediments together. Water filled with minerals such as calcite, iron oxide, and silica is squeezed out. The flowing water moves into the small spaces between the sediments. When the minerals in this water harden, the layers are **cemented** together, forming sedimentary rock. This sedimentary rock is laid down in layers called **strata**.

The effects of erosion are clearly visible along this section of California's Pacific Coast (above), while limestone strata from the Paleozoic Era can be seen along this cliff face near Alamogordo, New Mexico (below). The Paleozoic Era lasted from approximately 545 million years ago to 245 million years ago.

Sedimentary rock is placed into three major groups: **clastic**, **biogenic**, and **chemical**. Clastic rock is made up of pieces from other rocks, such as clay, silt, sand, and gravel. Sandstone comes from grains of sand that have been cemented together. It can be soft enough to crush into powder or, if it's cemented with silica, hard enough to use for building. Shale is made primarily out of clay. Conglomerate is a mixture of pebbles in a matrix, or cement foundation, of mud or sand.

Biogenic rock is formed from the remains of animals and/or plants that

Rock Not Lich-en This

Lichen (pronounced LIKE-un), a plant that is a partnership of algae and fungus, thrives on rocks. Lichen release acids that break down rock, allowing them to feed on the minerals inside.

have been compacted and cemented together. An example is **coal**. As trees and plants in freshwater swamps die, they sink to the bottom and begin to decay. Over millions of years, layers of mud and silt build up on the decomposing material, called **peat**. The pressure caused by the weight of the layers slowly squeezes out the oxygen, hydrogen, and nitrogen molecules. Gradually, the peat is transformed into hard mounds of coal. Coal is one of the few rocks that can catch fire. As it burns, the coal releases the energy of the plants that formed it millions of years before, which is why coal is called a **fossil fuel**. Limestone is one of the most common types of biogenic rock. It is made from the calcium carbonate shells of single-celled, microscopic animals. The shells of clams, snails, and oysters also occasionally form limestone. The White Cliffs of Dover in England and the Rock of Gibraltar, which rises 1,396 feet (426 m) out of the sea near the southern tip of Spain, are made of limestone.

Rock Talk

Rocks are named based on the size of their grains. Clay is made of particles almost too small to see that feel smooth. Silt, also made of tiny particles, feels gritty to the touch. Grains of sand have a gritty texture, are easily visible, and measure up to 0.08 inches (0.03 millimeters) in diameter.

Gravel consists of small grains larger than sand. It is divided into three categories: pebbles, which measure 0.08 to 2 inches (0.03 to 64 mm); cobbles, which measure 2 to 10 inches (64 to 256 mm); and boulders, which are larger than 10 inches (25 centimeters) in diameter.

Chemical sedimentary rock is formed when mineral-rich water evaporates, or turns from a liquid into gas. The evaporating water leaves mineral deposits bchind, which harden into rock. Evaporating water may leave behind rock salt. Inside limestone caves, calcium-rich water drips from cavern walls to create eerie rock icicles called stalactites and stalagmites. Other types of chemical sedimentary rocks include chalcedony, agate, and gypsum.

Anthracite coal is a metamorphic rock that is the hardest form of coal. Almost all of the anthracite coal in the United States is found in eastern Pennsylvania.

Ever-Changing Metamorphic Rock

Metamorphic rocks are those that begin as one kind of rock and end up another. *Meta* means "change" and *morph* means "form." Deep within Earth's crust, high heat and pressure can cause minerals inside a rock to change form, reacting with one another to create new minerals. Other elements may also be added by water and gases, producing new minerals. Metamorphic rocks often get folded, flattened, or smashed, yet they do not get hot enough to melt (or they would become igneous rocks).

Metamorphic rock can form from igneous rock, sedimentary rock, and other types of metamorphic rock. For instance, clay sediments put under pressure for many years form the sedimentary rock shale. Under more pressure and heat, shale, in turn, becomes the metamorphic rock slate. Additional pressure and heat cause mica crystals in the rock to grow, turning the slate into phyllite and then, eventually, the phyllite into schist. Similarly, limestone changes to marble, sandstone becomes quartzite, and granite forms first schist and then gneiss.

The Changing Face of Rock

In the late eighteenth century, Scottish geologist James Hutton realized that Earth's crust and surface were ever so slowly and continuously changing. Until then, most scientists believed that only major events, such as earthquakes or floods, could alter the shape of the land. But Hutton found that igneous, sedimentary, and metamorphic rocks are connected by geologic forces that are constantly at work, changing the makeup and structure of rocks. For instance, igneous rock that undergoes weathering, transportation, and deposition may cement to become sedimentary rock, which, in turn, may be buried and subjected to high heat and pressure to become metamorphic rock.

Not all rock follows the same geologic path. Many shortcuts can be taken. Igneous rock may not undergo weathering and erosion at the surface, but may remain deep

Rocks of Ages

Rocks more than 3.5 billion years old have been found on every continent. One of Earth's oldest rocks is located in Canada's Northwest Territories, a 4-billion-year-old metamorphic gneiss that scientists believe was once granite. Older still are the single zircon crystals found in young sedimentary rock in western Australia. At 4.3 billion years old, the tiny crystals are, so far, the oldest known material on the planet, almost as old as Earth itself.

underground to be heated and pressed into metamorphic rock. Likewise, sedimentary and metamorphic rock may be exposed at the surface, becoming the ingredients for a new mixture of sedimentary rock.

This geologist is loading a rock sample into a scientific instrument known as a cryogenic magnetometer, which will measure the rock's magnetism.

Chapter Four

Hot on the Mineral Trail

Geologists are a bit like detectives when it comes to discovering mineral deposits in Earth's crust. Whether exploring for veins of gold in South Africa or seams of coal in the United States, geologists use many tools in their search, or **geologic survey**.

A **gravimeter** measures the strength of gravity over areas of land. Since gold, copper, iron, and uranium are dense, they often register on the meter as tiny increases in gravitational pull. **Seismic**

The Kimberley diamond mine in the African nation of Namibia is one of the world's richest sources of diamonds.

A Diamond in the Rough

Several tons of kimberlite rock must be mined to find only a few gem-quality diamonds.

surveys are tools that send shock waves through the rock strata under land or on the ocean floor. Some of the layers let the waves pass through, while others reflect them back to the surface. How the rock reacts helps geologists map the strata and what type of minerals can be found in them. A **magnetometer** can pick up small variations in Earth's magnetic field to reveal deposits, or **ores**, of magnetic minerals such as iron. Some metals, such as uranium and plutonium, are radioactive. Airplanes equipped with **Geiger counters** that seek out these radioactive materials fly over areas. Similarly, electromagnetic coils can be placed on the ground to find minerals that carry electric current. A chemical survey tests lakes or rivers to see what kind of minerals may be seeping into the water. Soil and plant samples are also taken. Space satellites orbiting Earth take photographs of the planet and bounce radio waves off its surface to create radar maps of a wide area. Satellite views can help geologists find rock formations such as kimberlite pipes, primary sources of diamonds.

Once the geologic survey is complete, a narrow core is drilled into the ground. Samples are analyzed to make sure geologists have found the type of ore they have been looking for. Then mining companies mine the minerals.

Surface or **strip mining** is used to gather minerals such as aluminum and coal that are near the surface. Power shovels push away the top 30 to 90 feet (9 to 27 m) of soil to expose the coal, which is then dug out with smaller shovels. Copper and diamonds are usually extracted from **open-pit mines**, deep holes that may extend several thousand feet into the ground. The mine is created in layered sections called benches. As each layer is mined, a new one is dug. Finding veins of metals such as lead, nickel, and gold often means digging deep mines a mile or more into the ground. Tunnels take the miners deep underground, where rock is blasted away with explosives to expose the minerals.

The Human Touch

Many countries around the world depend on mining to support their economies, but extracting rocks and minerals from the ground can take a serious toll on the environment. Roads

This photograph of an open-pit iron-ore mine in Thabazimbi, South Africa, shows the type of damage such mining does to the surrounding landscape.

must be built, forests cleared, and wildlife disturbed. Large masses of rock must be mined to find and remove only small amounts of minerals. Miners often use poisonous chemicals to extract copper, gold, and silver from surrounding rock, putting themselves and others in danger. Rivers and streams are at risk of pollution from these toxic chemicals.

In Indonesia, miners often intrude on protected rainforests, using high-powered water hoses to flush gold out of the soil. They spray toxic mercury to bind the gold together while washing away nutrient-rich soil, destroying plants, and contaminating the waters. The story is similar in places such as Africa, Russia, Eastern Europe, and South America. In the Amazon rainforest, the mercury used to extract gold has leached into water supplies and the food chain of local villages. There is concern that the contamination may be linked to an increase in birth defects in some areas.

Cyanide, a chemical so dangerous that an amount the size of a grain of rice can kill a human, is also used around the world

Digging Up Danger

For more than a century, gold, silver, copper, and zinc were taken from Iron Mountain in Redding, California. The mine closed in 1963, yet Iron Mountain is still so polluted with mining chemicals that the water there is a thousand times more acidic than battery acid. Should this water, which once ate away a steel shovel that was left in a puddle, ever find its way into the Sacramento River, it would pollute the drinking water of Redding's 80,000 residents. So far, taxpayers have paid $150 million in clean-up costs.

to extract gold from rock. In January of 2000, 20,000 tons of cyanide-laced waste spilled from a gold mine in Oradea, Romania, polluting the Danube and Tisza Rivers for hundreds of miles. More than 1,200 tons of fish and wildlife were killed. In the United States, cyanide spills in California, Nevada, New Mexico, and Arizona have also harmed rivers and wildlife. In 1998, according to the U.S. Environmental Protection Agency (EPA), mining companies in the United States released 3.5 billion pounds (1.6 billion kg) of toxic chemicals into the environment.

Old, abandoned mines in the United States also present an environmental danger. In 1872, to encourage economic growth in the West, Congress passed the General Mining Law. The law allowed miners to take minerals from public lands at low cost. The law helped settle the West, but more than one hundred years of unrestricted mining left its scars on the landscape.

Geologists measure rock strata at a bulldozer cut in Tule Springs, Nevada.

Scientists estimate that 16,000 miles (25,000 km) of rivers, streams, and lakes are contaminated. Abandoned mines across the nation may number in the millions, although no one can agree on exactly how many there are.

In the past several decades, environmental awareness

Protecting the Planet

Before the Surface Mining Law, which President Jimmy Carter signed in 1977, coal mining companies in the United States did not have to consider their impact on fish, forests, and wildlife. Now these environmental concerns must be addressed and reclamation plans spelled out before mining can begin.

around the world has helped create new mining restrictions. Many countries, including the United States, now require companies to complete an **environmental impact statement (EIS)** before mining. An EIS predicts how a project will affect natural resources such as air, water, land, and wildlife. The mining company must outline plans to restore, or reclaim, the land once they are finished. Some of these **reclamation** steps include refilling strip mines and covering them with topsoil and plants, treating and filtering water used in processing before releasing it into rivers, and turning open-pit mines into natural water reservoirs. Sometimes, reclaimed mine sites are turned into productive farmland, pastureland, or residential neighborhoods.

Chapter Five

Where Do You Stand?

As the world's population tops 6 billion, scientists say we are beginning to see signs that humans are depleting the resources we have come to rely on for everything from pencils to plastics. Mining companies must now tap into less productive ores to get minerals, creating further waste and harm to the environment. Yet a growing population that will likely reach 10 billion before the middle of the century is demanding more and more natural resources. In the United

States, each person, on average, uses about 40,000 pounds (18,400 kg) of minerals every year.

Where do you stand? If you agree that it's important to conserve natural resources, would you be willing to change your own habits? Could you accept having fewer choices when it came to toys, computer games, or electronics if it meant saving some of Earth's resources? Would your parents be willing not to buy a new car quite as often if it meant conserving metals and plastics?

Once rocks and minerals are taken from the ground they are also forever removed from the rock cycle. That is why many scientists and environmental activists stress the importance of **reusing** and recycling products. Reusing means not throwing out products after their first use. Buying water containers at the grocery store that can be refilled or rechargeable batteries is a way to reuse. Recycling takes product packaging and breaks it down so it can be reprocessed into new materials. Aluminum, glass, and some plastics can be melted down and made into new soda cans, bottles, and containers over and over again.

Here are some more things you can do to make a difference in conserving Earth's resources.

- At home, recycle glass bottles, soda cans, paper, newspaper, and plastics. If your neighborhood doesn't have a curbside recycle program (almost half of the United States doesn't), drop off your recyclables at brightly colored bins, or "igloos," near shopping centers.

Country of Consumers

Although the United States is home to about 5 percent of the world's population, its residents consume 33 percent of the available materials on Earth, far more than any other nation on the planet.

Most communities in the United States now encourage recycling.

- Save plastic grocery bags. You can bring them to the grocery store on your next trip to use again. Better yet, use cloth bags for carrying groceries home.
- Reduce the number of products you buy that have too much unnecessary packaging.
- Reuse foam packing "peanuts" and bubble wrap that comes in the mail.
- Instead of throwing away old clothes, toys, or furniture, donate them to a local charity.

For more recycling tips, log on to the EPA's Web site at *http://www.epa.gov/kids.* If you're interested in finding out more about a career in geology, visit your local library or explore the U.S. Geologic Survey's Web site at *http://www.usgs.gov.*

Billions of years have created majestic rock formations, valuable minerals, and amazing gems. By protecting the rocks under our feet and conserving what we hold in our hands, humans can help keep the rock cycle flowing on its timeless journey.

47

Glossary

alloy—a mixture of two types of metals or a mixture of a metal and a nonmetal

atom—the smallest part of an element

basalt—the most common type of volcanic igneous rock

batholith—a large mass of igneous rock, usually made of granite, with an exposed surface of more than 60 square miles (100 sq km)

biogenic rock—a type of sedimentary rock created by living organisms, their remains, or activities; examples are coal and limestone

cementation—a process in which rock fragments are bound together to make solid sedimentary rock

chemical compound—the substance that results from the bonding of two or more elements

chemical rock—a type of sedimentary rock formed by the evaporation of mineral-rich water; gypsum and rock salt are examples of chemical rock

chemical weathering—the breakdown of solid rock through chemical process

clastic rock—a type of sedimentary rock made up of fragments of broken rocks that have been eroded, transported, and deposited; sandstone, shale, and conglomerate are types of clastic rock

coal—a biogenic sedimentary rock formed from fossilized plant remains

crystal—a solid mineral body, often transparent, with a distinct atomic structure

crystal form—the geometric shape formed by a mineral that is determined by its atomic structure

deposition—the laying down of rock fragments that have been transported by erosional forces

element—a substance that cannot be broken into simpler substances by chemical means; alone or combined, elements form minerals

environmental impact statement (EIS)—A formal study that indicates how a development or project will affect natural resources such as air, water, land, and wildlife

erosion—the transportation of material such as rock from its original location by forces such as wind, water, ice, and gravity

fossil—the remains of any organism that once lived that are usually chemically altered and preserved in some way

fossil fuel—any naturally occurring hydrocarbon fuel formed underground by the action of pressure on the remains of dead plants and animals; coal, oil, natural gas, and peat are fossil fuels

Geiger counter—an instrument used to detect and measure radioactive particles within a substance

geologic or **rock cycle**—the loop that may be followed by one or more elements as they circulate through Earth's crust

geologic survey—an exploration for Earth's natural resources using tools such as electromagnetic coils, Geiger counters, magnetometers, chemical tests, and satellite photos

geologist—a scientist who studies the origin, structure, and composition of Earth and other planets

granite—one of the most common types of plutonic igneous rock on Earth, composed mainly of quartz, feldspar, and mica

gravimeter—an instrument that measures slight variations in Earth's gravitational field that may be used to locate metal ores underground

igneous rock—one of the three main groups of rock; it is formed as magma cools and hardens on or below the surface of Earth

impurities—trace amounts of one or more elements that tint a crystal

lava—hot melted rock (magma) that has reached the surface of Earth

luster—the way the surface of a mineral reflects light

magma—hot, melted rock beneath Earth's surface that contains suspended crystals and dissolved gases

magma chamber—a reservoir in which magma accumulates before being emptied on to Earth's surface through a volcano

magnetometer—an instrument that measures the strength of Earth's magnetic field and is often used to detect magnetic minerals beneath the surface

matrix—the mass of rock in which crystals are set

metamorphic rock—one of the three main groups of rock; it is formed from any of the three types of rock when they are subjected to heat, pressure and/or chemical changes

mineral—a naturally occurring substance that has a definite chemical composition

Mohs Scale—a scale of mineral hardness, from 1 to 10, created by mineralogist Freidrich Mohs to aid in the identification of minerals

open-pit mine—a large, open crater dug into the surface of Earth from which minerals are extracted

ore—a naturally occurring deposit from which a useful product; such as metal, can be extracted

organic matter—dead plants and animals

peat—a mass of partly decomposed plant debris

physical weathering—the breakdown of solid rock through mechanical forces, such as wind, heat, and water

plutonic rock—igneous rock formed from cooled magma inside Earth's crust

properties—the characteristics of a mineral defined by its atomic structure; color, streak, and hardness are some of the properties of a mineral

reclamation—in mining, restoring land that has been mined to its previous condition or converting it to another productive use

reuse—to use a product or product packaging more than once

recycling—breaking down and reprocessing material into new products; glass, paper, and aluminum are recyclable

rhyolite—a type of volcanic igneous rock

rock—one mineral, several minerals, and/or a combination of minerals and organic substances in solid form; Earth's rocks are classified into three main groups: igneous, sedimentary, and metamorphic

sedimentary rock—one of the three main groups of rock; it is formed through the erosion, transportation, deposition, and cementation of pre-existing rocks; sedimentary rocks are classified as clastic, biogenic, or chemical

seismic survey—an instrument that sends shock waves into the ground or seafloor to determine the composition of the rock strata in them

silicate—any mineral that contains the elements oxygen and silicon (SiO_4); silicates comprise one-third of all minerals and 90 percent of Earth's crust

stratum (plural strata)—a layer of sedimentary rock

streak—a colored mark left when a mineral is rubbed across a piece of unglazed porcelain, which is commonly used to identify the mineral

surface or **strip mining**—a method of mining in which soil and vegetation is removed to expose minerals close to the planet's surface

volcanic glass—obsidian rock, which is created when lava on the surface of Earth cools too quickly for any crystals to form

volcanic rock—a type of rock that forms when lava cools and solidifies on the surface of Earth

To Find Out More

Books

Burton, Jane and Kim Taylor. *The Nature and Science of Rocks.* Milwaukee, Wisconsin: Gareth Stevens Publishing, 1998.

Discovery Channel. *Rocks and Minerals.* New York: Discovery Books, 1999.

Downs, Sandra. *Earth's Hidden Treasures.* Brookfield, Connecticut: Millbrook Press, Twenty-First Century Books, 1999.

Fuller, Sue. *Rocks and Minerals.* New York: Dorling Kindersley, 1995.

Javna, John. *Fifty Simple Things Kids Can Do to Save the Earth.* New York: Earth Works Group, 1999.

Kittinger, Jo S. *A Look at Rocks: From Coal to Kimberlite*. New York: Franklin Watts, 1997.

Lawton, Rebecca, Diane Lawton, and Susan Panttaja. *Discover Nature: In the Rocks, Things to Know and Do*. Mechanicsburg, Pennsylvania: Stackpole Books, 1997.

Videos

The Grand Canyon, PBS Nature Series Video, 2000.

Modern Marvels: Mount Rushmore, The History Channel, 2000.

Rocks & Minerals, Dorling Kindersley, Eyewitness Video, 1996.

The World's Deepest Goldmine, Discovery Channel, 2001.

CD-ROM

Earthquest (Windows & MacIntosh), Dorling Kindersley, 1997.

Online Sites and Places to Visit

American Museum of Natural History
79th Street and Central Park West

New York, NY
(212) 313-7278
http://www.amnh.org/exhibitions/diamonds
Explore how diamonds are formed and blown to the surface through volcanic eruptions. Visit the Museum's Hall of Minerals in New York City to see more than 100,000 rocks, minerals, and gems in its collection, including the Star of India, the world's largest blue-star sapphire.

Mineralogical Society of America
1015 18th Street NW, Suite 601
Washington, DC 20036
http://www.minsocam.org
Have a question about rocks and minerals? Ask a mineralogist online at the MSA website. Also, discover more about collecting and identify rocks at the *Minerals 4 Kids* education page.

Mount Rushmore National Memorial
PO Box 268
Keystone, SD 57751-0268
(605) 574-2523
http://www.nps.gov/moru
Discover how Mount Rushmore in South Dakota was designed and sculpted. See for yourself how the cliff took shape and learn why some of its features were never completed.

National Museum of Natural History
Smithsonian Institution
10th Street and Constitution Avenue, NW
Washington, DC 20560-0166
(202) 357-4548
http://www.nmnh.si.edu/minsci
See photos of some of the amazing rocks, gems, and minerals on display at the Smithsonian, such as the Hope Diamond and Star of Asia sapphire. The museum is home to more than 375,000 gem and mineral specimens.

U.S. Geological Survey
Minerals Information
12201 Sunrise Valley Drive
Reston, Virginia 20192
1-888-275-8747
http://www.usgs.gov
http://ask.usgs.gov
Learn about gold prospecting, starting your own rock or gem collection, and how to protect the environment at this Web site. You can also ask a geologist a question online and find out more about the different types of rocks found on Earth.

A Note on Sources

In exploring the world of rocks and minerals, I consulted scientists at the U.S. Geologic Survey, the Mineralogical Society of America, and the Smithsonian Institution in Washington, DC. I relied on these and other experts for the most current information and analysis of the topic area. Special thanks to Dr. Elizabeth Nesbitt, Curator of Invertebrate Paleontology at the Burke Museum of Natural History and Culture at the University of Washington in Seattle, who so graciously offered knowledge, insight, and direction.

My research also included reading numerous books on the topic, including textbooks, guidebooks, and works written for young readers. Magazine articles, newspaper features, and video documentaries rounded out my investigation.

Because I believe it is critical to impart a balanced view of the global impact of the topic, I gathered information on mining, consumerism, and recycling from the U.S. Environmental Protection Agency, U.S. Bureau of Land Management, U.S. Office of Surface Mining, The Nature Conservancy, and the Sierra Club. I also read books such as *Earth in the Balance* by Al Gore, *Earthday Guide to Planet Repair* by Denis Hayes, and *The Earth Around Us: Maintaining a Livable Planet* edited by Jill S. Schneiderman, which is a collection of environmental essays written by prominent scientists.

Finally, I made firsthand observations whenever possible. Whether strolling through a museum to view stunning specimens of jade, topaz, and opal (my favorite gem) or searching for agates along the rocky beaches along the Washington coast, nature's creations are an endless source of wonder for those of us who are rock lovers at heart.

—*Trudi Strain Trueit*

Index

Numbers in *italics* indicate illustrations.

Agate, 35
Alloys, 17
Aluminum, 9, 14, 17
Amethyst, 20, 21
Apatite, *22*, 25

Barium, 13
Basalt, 31
Batholiths, 29
Beryl, 19, 20
Biogenic rock, 33, 34
Brass, 17
Bronze, 17

Calcite, 19, *22*, 25, 33
Carbon, 34
Chalcedony, 35
Chemical compounds, 14
Chemical weathering, 32
Chemical rock, 33
Chromium, 21

Citrine, 20
Clastic rock, 33
Clay, 33, 34, 36
Coal, 34
Conglomerate, 33
Copper, 13, 17, 39, 41, 42
Corundum, 19, 20, 21, 25
Crystals, 14, 19, 21
Cyanide, 42, 43

Deposition, 33
Diamond, 9, 19, 20, 24, 25,
    40, 41
Diorite, 29

Emerald, 20
Erosion, 32, 36

Feldspar, 16–17
Fireworks, *12*, 13–14
Fluorite, 19, *22*, 25

Fossil fuel, 34

Gabbro, 29
Gems, 9, 19–24
Geologic cycle, 10–11
Geologists, 11, 26, 39–40
Giant's Causeway, 31
Gold, 9, 17, 39, 41, 42
Gneiss, 19, 36, 37
Granite, *26*, 29, 36, 37
Graphite, 19
Gravel, 33, 34
Gravimeter, 39
Great Pyramid, 7–9, *8*
Great Wall of China, 9–10, *10*
Gypsum, 19, *22*, 25, 35

Igneous rock, 28–32
Iron, 9, 14, 17, 21, 33, 39, 40

Kimberlite, *24*, 40

Lava, 30, 31
Lead, 9, 17, 41
Lichen, 34
Limestone, 19, 34, 35, 36
Louvre museum, *6*, 10
Luster, 24

Magma, 28–29

Magnesium, 14
Magnetometers, *38*, 39, 40
Marble, 19, 36
Mercury, *17*, 42
Metamorphic rock, 28, 35–37
Mica, 16, 17, 36
Minerals
    durability of, 24–25
    properties of, 13–26
    uses of, 9, 13–26
Mining, 40–44
Mohs, Friedrich, 24
Mohs Scale, 24–25

Obsidian, 31
Olivine, 20
Opal, 20
Ores, 40
Organic matter, 16
Orthoclase, *23*, 25

Peat, 34
Peridot, 20
Peridotite, 29
Phyllite, 36
Physical weathering, 32
Platinum, 17
Plutonic rock, 28–29
Plutonium, 40
Pollution, 42–44

Potassium, 14

Quartz, 16, 17, 20, 21, *23*, 25
Quartzite, 36

Reclamation, 44
Recycling, 10–11, 46–47
Rhyolite, 30
Rock cycle, 10–11, 46
Rocks,
    classification of, 27–28
    creation of, 28–37
    uses of, 9–11
Ruby, 20, 21

Sand, 27, 33, 34
Sapphire, 20
Schist, 19, 36
Sedimentary rock, 28, 32–35
Seismic surveys, 39
Shale, 33, 36
Silica, 33
Silicate, 16
Silicon, 14, 16
Silt, 33, 34
Silver, 17, 41, 42

Sodium, 13, 14
Stalactites, 35
Stalagmites, 35
Stonehenge, 9, *10*
Strata, 33
Streak, 23
Strontium, 13
Sulfur, 19
Syenite, 29
Sylvite, 19

Talc, 25
Titanium, 21
Topaz, 20, *23*
Tourmaline, 16

Uranium, 17, 39, 40

Volcanoes, 28–29
Volcanic glass, 31
Volcanic rock, 30, 31

Weathering, 36

Zinc, 17, 42
Zircon, 37

About the Author

Trudi Strain Trueit is an award-winning broadcast journalist and writer who combines her love of rock collecting with a fascination with the history and folklore of Earth's treasures. Her adventures have led her to writing books and articles about nature, weather, and wildlife.

As a television news reporter and weather forecaster, she has contributed stories to ABC News, CBS News, and CNN. Ms. Trueit has written many books for the Franklin Watts Library Series. Her titles include *Clouds*; *Earthquakes*; *Fossils*; *Rain, Hail, and Snow*; *Storm Chasers*; *The Water Cycle*; and *Volcanoes*. She is also the author of *Octopuses, Squids, and Cuttlefish* in Scholastic's Animals in Order series. Ms. Trueit earned a B.A. in broadcast journalism. She makes her home in Everett, Washington, with her husband, Bill.